OUTLINES
OF
INDIAN PHILOSOPHY:

OUTLINES

OF

INDIAN PHILOSOPHY:

WITH AN APPENDIX

ON THE PHILOSOPHY OF THE VEDANTA

IN ITS

RELATIONS TO OCCIDENTAL METAPHYSICS

PAUL DEUSSEN

GYAN

Published by

GYAN

Gyan Publishing House
5, Ansari Road
Daryaganj, New Delhi-110002
Phone: 011-47034999, 9811692060
E-mail: books@gyanbooks.com

Distribution Network
gyanbooks.com
India, USA, Canada, UK, Australia

ISBN: 978-93-6920-026-9 (HB)

First Published, 1907

2nd Impression 2025

Printed at: Gyan Press, Delhi.

OUTLINES OF INDIAN PHILOSOPHY
Author: PAUL DEUSSEN

OUTLINES
OF
INDIAN PHILOSOPHY

OUTLINES

OF

INDIAN PHILOSOPHY

WITH AN APPENDIX

ON THE PHILOSOPHY OF THE VEDÂNTA

IN ITS

RELATIONS TO OCCIDENTAL METAPHYSICS

BY

DR. PAUL DEUSSEN

PROFESSOR AT THE UNIVERSITY OF KIEL

BERLIN

KARL CURTIUS

1907

PREFATORY NOTES
BY THE AUTHOR

The first of the two treatises, composing this little volume, appeared in the Indian Antiquary 1902 and is reprinted here with the kind permission of the editor Sir Richard Temple. The appendix "On the Philosophy of the Vedânta" was originally an address delivered before the Bombay Branch of the Royal Asiatic Society, the 25th February 1893.

Both treatises complete in some way each other, the first being a very short summary of the history of the Indian philosophy, the second giving a concise idea of that religious and philosophical system, which more than any other is ruling in India even in our days.

A fuller account of the subjects treated in this little volume may be found in the following works of the same author:

Allgemeine Geschichte der Philosophie mit besonderer Berücksichtigung der Religionen, vol. I: Allgemeine Einleitung und Philosophie des

Veda bis auf die Upanishads, vol. II: Die Philosophie der Upanishads (translated into English by Rev. A. S. Geden under the title: The Philosophy of the Upanishads, Edinburgh 1906); vol. III: (in preparation) Die nachvedische Philosophie der Inder. The second edition of the volumes published till now appeared Leipzig, 1906 and 1907.

Sechzig Upanishads des Veda, aus dem Sanskrit übersetzt und mit Einleitungen und Anmerkungen versehen, II^d edition Leipzig, 1905. —

Vier philosophische Texte des Mahâbhâratam, aus dem Sanskrit übersetzt, Leipzig 1906.

Die Sûtra's des Vedânta nebst dem vollständigen Kommentare des Çaṅkara, aus dem Sanskrit übersetzt, Leipzig 1887.

Das System des Vedânta, nach den Brahma-Sûtra's des Bâdarâyaṇa und dem Kommentare des Çaṅkara über dieselben als ein Compendium der Dogmatik des Brahmanismus vom Standpunkte des Çaṅkara aus dargestellt. II^d edition Leipzig 1906. —

CONTENTS

I. OUTLINES OF INDIAN PHILOSOPHY.

II. ON THE PHILOSOPHY OF THE VEDÂNTA IN ITS RELATIONS TO OCCIDENTAL METAPHYSICS.

OUTLINES
OF INDIAN PHILOSOPHY

PREFATORY REMARKS

AMONG the pretexts by which European idleness tries to escape the study of Indian philosophy we hear most frequently the remark that the philosophy of the Indians is quite different from our own and has nothing whatever to do with the development of Occidental religion and philosophy. The fact is perfectly true; but far from being a reason for neglecting the study of Indian wisdom, it furnishes us with the strongest argument in favour of devoting ourselves to it all the more. The philosophy of the Indians must become for every one who takes any interest in the investigation of philosophical truth, an object of the highest interest; for Indian philosophy is and will be the only possible parallel to what so far the Europeans have considered as philosophy. In fact, modern European philosophy has sprung from the scholasticiom of the Middle Ages; medieval thought again is a product of Greek philosophy on the one hand and of the Biblical dogma on the other. The doctrine of the Bible has again its roots in part in the oldest Semitic creed and in part in the

Importance of Indian Philosophy

Persian religion of Zoroaster, which, as an intermediate link between the Old and the New Testament, has exercised more influence than is commonly attributed to it. In this way the whole of European thought from Pythagoras and Xenophanes, from Moses and Zoroaster, through Platonism and Christianity down to the Kantian and post-Kantian philosophy, forms a complex of ideas, whose elements are variously related to and dependent on each other. On the other hand Indian philosophy through all the centuries of its development has taken its course uninfluenced by West-Asiatic and European thought; and precisely for this reason the comparison of European philosophy with that of the Indians is of the highest interest. Where both agree the presumption is that their conclusions are correct, no less than in a case where two calculators working by different methods arrive at the same result; and where Indian and European views differ it is an open question on which side the truth is probably to be found.

Periods of Indian Philosophy

2. Indian philosophy falls naturally into three periods; these three periods are equally strongly marked in the general history of Indian civilisation and are dependent on the geography of India. India, as Sir William Jones has already remarked, has the form of a square whose four angles are turned to the four cardinal points, and

are marked by the Hindu Kush in the north, Cape Comorin in the south, and the mouths of the Ganges and Indus in the east and west. If a line be drawn from the mouth of the Indus to that of the Ganges (nearly coinciding with the tropic of Cancer), the square is divided into two triangles — Hindustan in the north, and the Deccan in the south. If again in the northern triangle we let fall a perpendicular from the vertex upon the base, this divides northern India into the valley of the Indus and the plain of the Ganges, separated by the desert of Marusthala. Thus India falls into three parts — (1) the Panjab, (2) the plain of the Ganges, (3) the Deccan plateau. To these three geographical divisions correspond the three periods of Indian life: — (1) The domain of the Aryan Hindus in the oldest period was limited to the valley of the Indus with its five tributaries; the only literary monuments of this epoch are the 1017 hymns of the Ṛigveda. Though chiefly serving religious purposes they give by the way a lively and picturesque delineation of that primitive manner of life in which there were no castes, no *âçramas* (stages of life), and no Brahmanical order of life in general. The hymns of the Ṛigveda display not only the ancient Indian polytheism in its full extent, but contain also in certain of the later hymns the first germs of a philosophical view of the world. (2) It may have been about 1000 B. C. that the Aryans starting from the Panjab began to extend their conquests to the east and occupied little by little the plain extending from the Himâlayas in the north and the Vindhyas in the south to the mouth of the Ganges. The conquest of this territory may have been accomplished, roughly speaking, between 1000 and 500 B. C. As literary monuments of this second period of Indian life we find the *Saṃhitâs* of the *Yajur-*, *Sâma-*, and *Atharvaveda*, together with the Brâhmaṇas and their culmination in the Upanishads. Hand in hand with this literary development we have under the spiritual dominion of the Brahmans the establishment of that original organisation which as the Brahmanical order of life has survived in India with some modification until the present day. (3) After these two periods, which we may distinguish as "old-Vedic" and "new-Vedic", follows a third period of Indian history — the "post-Vedic" — beginning about 500 B. C. with the rise of the heretical tendencies of Buddhism and Jainism, and producing in the succeeding centuries a large number of literary works in which, together with poetry, grammar, law, medicine and astronomy, a rich collection of philosophical works in Sanskrit permits us to trace the development of the philosophical mind down to the present time. In this period Indian, *i. e.*, Brahmanical, civilisation makes its way round the coast of Southern India and Ceylon and penetrates conquering into the remotest districts of Central India.

FIRST PERIOD

PHILOSOPHY OF THE ṚIGVEDA

3. The oldest interpretation of Nature and therefore the first philosophy of a people is its religion, and for the origin and essence of religion there is no book in the world more instructive than the Ṛigveda; Homer in Greece, and the most ancient parts of the Old Testament show religion in an advanced state of development which presupposes many preliminary stages now lost to us. In India alone we can trace back religion to its first origin. It is true that the hymns of the Ṛigveda also show religion in a later stage of development; some primitive gods stand already in the background, as Dyaus (heaven) and Pṛithivî (earth); they are rarely mentioned but with an awe which shows their high position at an earlier period. Another god, Varuna (the starry heaven), is still prominent, but even he is in danger of being superseded by Indra, the god of the thunderstorm and of war; and a remarkable hymn (iv. 42)

Religion of the Ṛigveda

exhibits a dialogue between Varuna and Indra, in which each boasts his greatness, while the poet notwithstanding the full respect for Varuna, betrays a certain partiality for Indra. This case and many others show that the Ṛigvedic religion also is in an advanced state of development; but the names of the gods considered etymologically and the character of the myths related of them, are so transparent that we are able in nearly every case to discover the original meaning of the god in question. Thus there can be no doubt that Varuṇa (*'Ουρανός*) is a personification of the heaven with its regular daily revolution, and that he only in later times became a god of the waters. Other gods represent the sun in its various aspects: Sûrya the radiant globe of the sun, Savitar the arouser, Vishṇu the vivifying force, Mitra the benevolent light, the friend of mankind, and Pûshan, the shepherd of the world. Besides these we have the two Açvins, a divine pair who bring help in time of need, and seem to mean originally the twilight with which the day begins and the terrors of the night have an end. A very transparent personification of the dawn is Ushas (*'Ηώς*, Aurora) represented as a beautiful maiden displaying every morning her charms before the eyes of the world. If from these gods of the luminous heaven we pass to the second part of the universe, the atmosphere, we meet here among others Vâyu or Vâta, god of the winds, Parjanya, the rain-god, the terrible

Rudra, who probably personifies the destructive and purifying lightning, further the Maruts, the merry gods of the storm and above all Indra, the god of the thunderstorm, who in his battles against the demons that hinder the rain from falling, is the typical god of warfare and thus the ideal of the Hindu of the heroic epoch. Lastly, coming to the earth, there are many phenomena of Nature and life considered as divine powers, but above all Agni, god of the destructive and helpful fire, and Soma, a personification of the intoxicating power of the soma-drink, which inspires gods and men to heroic deeds. This short sketch shows clearly what the gods were in ancient India and what *mutatis mutandis* they are originally in every religion of the world, namely, personifications of natural forces and natural phenomena. Man in passing from the brute state to human consciousness found himself surrounded by and dependent on various natural powers: the nourishing earth, the fertilising heaven, the wind, the rain, the thunderstorm, etc., and ascribed to them not only will, like that of man, which was perfectly correct, but also human personality, human desires and human weaknesses, which certainly was wrong. These personified natural powers were further considered as the origin, the maintainers and controllers of what man found in himself as the moral law, opposed to the egoistic tendencies natural to man. Thus the religion of the Ṛigveda may teach us that gods, wherever we meet them in the world, are compounded of two elements—a mythological, so far as they are personifications of natural powers and phenomena, and a moral element so far as these personifications are considered as the authors and guardians of the moral law. Let us add that the better religion is that in which the moral element preponderates, and the less perfect religion that in which the mythological element is developed at the cost of the moral. If we apply this criterion to the religion of the Ṛigveda, we must recognize that, notwithstanding its high interest in so many respects, it cannot as a religion claim a specially high position; for the Ṛigvedic gods, though at the same time the guardians of morality *(gopâ ṛitasya)*, are mainly regarded as beings of superhuman powers but egotistic tendencies. This moral deficiency of the Ṛigvedic religion has certainly been the chief cause of the surprisingly rapid decay of the old-Vedic worship; this decay and at the same time the first germs of philosophical thought we can trace in certain of the later hymns of the Ṛigveda, as we shall now proceed to demonstrate.

Decay of the Old-Vedic Religion

4. In certain later hymns of the Ṛigveda there are unmistakeable signs that the ancient creed was falling into disrepute. A beautiful hymn (x. 117) recommends the duty of benevolence without any reference to the gods, apparently be-

cause they were too weak a support for pure moral actions. Another hymn (x. 151) is addressed not to a god but to Faith, and praising the merit of faith, concludes with the prayer: "O Faith, make us faithful." In a time of unshaken faith such a prayer would hardly have been offered. But we have clearer proofs that the old-Vedic faith began to fade. In a hymn (ii. 12) to Indra, the principal god of the Vedic Hindu, the poet says: — "the terrible god, whose existence they doubt, and ask 'where is he', nay, whom they deny, saying, 'he is not', this god will destroy his enemies like play-things" — and doubts like this occur now and then; but even more frequently we meet passages and entire hymns which evidently ridicule the gods and their worship, more especially that of the god Indra. Everybody in the world, says the hymn ix. 112, pursues his egoistic interests, the joiner hopes for broken wheels, the doctor for broken limbs, the blacksmith looks for customers; I am a poet, says the author, my father is a physician, my mother turns the mill in the kitchen, and so we all pursue our own advantage, as a herdsman his cows. This little piece of humorous poetry would be perfectly innocent were it not that after each verse comes the refrain, probably taken from an old hymn: "Thou, O Soma, flow for Indra", which evidently means that

Indra also seeks his own advantage and is an egotist like other people.

Even more bold is the scorn in hymn x. 119, which introduces Indra in the merriest humour, ready to give away everything, ready to destroy the earth and all that it contains, boasting of his greatness in ridiculous fashion, — all this because, as the refrain tells us, he is in an advanced stage of intoxication, caused by excessive appreciation of the soma offered to him. Another hymn (vii. 103) sings of the frogs, comparing their voices to the noise of a Brahmanical school and their hopping round the tank to the behaviour of drunken priests celebrating a nocturnal offering of Soma. As here the holy teachers and the priests, so in another hymn (x. 82) the religious poetry of the Veda and its authors are depreciated by the words: "The Vedic minstrels, wrapped in fog and floods of words, go on the stump to make a livelihood."

Beginnings of Philosophical Thought

5. The age in which such words were possible was certainly ripe for philosophy; and accordingly we see emerging in certain later hymns of the Ṛigveda the thought by which here as well as in Greece philosophy begins — the conception of the unity of the world. Just as Xenophanes in Greece puts above all the popular gods his one deity who is nothing more than the universe consi-

dered as a unity, we find in the Ṛigveda a remarkable seeking and enquiring after that one from which, as an eternal, unfathomable, unspeakable unity, all gods, worlds, and creatures originate. The Hindus arrive at this Monism by a method essentially different from that of other countries. Monotheism was attained in Egypt by a mechanical identification of the various local gods, in Palestine by proscription of other gods and violent persecution of their worshippers for the benefit of the national god, Jehovah. In India they reached Monism though not Monotheism on a more philosophical path, seeing through the veil of the manifold the unity which underlies it. Thus the profound and difficult hymn, i. 164, pointing out the difference of the names Agni, Indra and Vâyu, comes to the bold conclusion: "there is one being of which the poets of the hymns speak under various names." The same idea of the unity of the universe is expressed in the wonderful hymn x. 129, which as the most remarkable monument of the oldest philosophy we here translate: —

1. In the beginning there was neither Non-Being nor Being, neither atmosphere nor sky beyond. — What enveloped all things? Where were they, in whose care? What was the ocean, the unfathomable depth?

2. At that time there was neither mortal nor immortal, neither night nor day. — That being the only one, breathed without air in independence. Beyond it nought existed.

3. Darkness was there; by darkness enshrouded in the beginning, an ocean without lights was all this world; — but the pregnant germ which was enveloped by the husk was born by the strength of penitence.

4. And forth went as the first-born Kâma (love) which was the primordial seed of mind. — Thus wise men meditating have found out the link of Non-Being and Being in the heart.

5. They threw their plumbline across the universe. What was then below and what above? There were seedbearers; there was mighty striving; independence beneath, exertion above.

6. But who knows and who can tell from where was born, from where came forth creation? — The gods came afterwards into existence. Who then can say from whence creation came?

7. He from whom this creation proceeded, whether he created it or not, He whose eye watches it in the highest heaven, He perhaps knows it — or perhaps he knows it not.

I add a metrical translation[1]:

1. Non-Being was not; Being was not yet;
   There was no vault of heaven, no realm of air,
Where was the ocean, where the deep abyss?
   What mantled all? Where was it, in whose care?

2. Death was not known nor yet immortal life;
   Night was not born and day was not yet seen.
Airless he breathed in primevality
   The One beyond whom nought hath ever been.

3. Darkness prevailed at first, a chaos dread;
   'Twas this great world, clad in its cloak of night.
And then was brought to being the germ of all,
   The One pent in this husk, by *Tapas*' might.

4. And first of all from him proceeded love,
   Kâma, the primal seed and germ of thought.
In Non-existence was by sages found
   Existence' root, when in the heart they sought.

5. When through the realm of Being their arc they spanned,
   What was beneath it, what was in their ken?
Germ-carriers beneath! Strivings above!
   The seeds of things were hid, the things were seen.

---

[1] I am indebted for this translation to Mr. N. W. Thomas, M. A.

6. Whence sprang the universe? Who gave it form?
What eye hath seen its birth? Its source who knows?
Before the world was made the gods were not;
Who then shall tell us whence these things arose?

7. He who hath moulded and called forth the world,
Whether he hath created it or not,
Who gazeth down on it from heaven's heights,
He knoweth it; or doth he know it not?

Attempts to determine that Unity

6. The great thought of the unity of all things having been conceived, the next task was to find out what this unity was. For the attempt to determine it the hymn x. 121, is especially typical which, starting apparently from the hymn x. 129, or a similar piece of work, seeks a name for that unknown god who was the last unity of the universe. In the first eight verses the poet points out the wonders of creation and concludes each verse by asking "Who is that god, that we may worship him?" In the ninth verse he finds a name for that new and unknown deity, calling it Prajâpati (lord of the creatures). This name in striking contrast to the names of the old Vedic gods, is evidently not of popular origin but the creation of a philosophical thinker. Henceforth Prajâpati occupies the highest position in the pantheon, until he is displaced by two other, more

philosophical conceptions — Brahman and Âtman. These three names, Prajâpati, Brahman and Âtman dominate the whole philosophical development from the Ṛigveda to the Upanishads. The oldest term Prajâpati is merely mythological and the transition from it to the term Âtman (which, as we shall see, is highly philosophical) is very natural. But it is very characteristic of the Hindu mind that this transition is accomplished by means of an intermediate term Brahman, which was originally merely ritual in its meaning and application, signifying "prayer". At the time of the Upanishads the name Prajâpati is nearly forgotten and appears only now and then as a mythological figure, while the terms Brahman and Âtman have become identical and serve in turn to express that being which, as we shall see, is the only object of which the Upanishads treat. We have now to trace the history of these three terms in detail.

History of Prajâpati

7. It is characteristic of the way in which Indian religion developed that a mere philosophical abstraction such as Prajâpati might put in the background all the other gods and occupy in the time of the Brâhmaṇas the highest place in the Hindu pantheon. Prajâpati in this period is considered as the father of gods, men and demons, as the creator and ruler of the world. Numerous passages of the *Brâhmaṇas*, intended to recommend some ritual

usage, describe the rite or formula as produced by Prajâpati and employed by him in the creation of the world. Such passages regularly begin with the phrase that in the beginning Prajâpati alone was, that he performed penance and thereby worthily prepared himself for creating the different gods, the worlds and the various implements and materials of sacrifice. All the gods depend on him; in him they take refuge when harassed by the demons; and to him as arbitrator they come if some quarrel about their relative dignity arises. Into these details we will not enter; we will here only point out that the Indian idea of creation is essentially different from that current in the Christian world. Prajâpati does not create a world; he transforms himself, his body and his limbs into the different parts of the universe. Therefore in creating he is swallowed up, he falls to pieces, and is restored by the performance of some rite which is in this way recommended. In later texts we observe a tendency to get rid of Prajâpati whether by deriving him from a still higher principle, such as the primordial waters, the Non-ent preceding his existence, or by explaining him away and identifying him with the creating mind, the creating word, the sacrifice or the year as principles of the world. In older passages Prajâpati creates, among other ritual objects, the Brahman; later passages on the other hand make him dependent on the Brahman.

8. Every attempt to explain this central idea of Indian philosophy must proceed from the fact that the word Brahman throughout the Ṛigveda in which it occurs more than 200 times, signifies without exception nothing more than "prayer". Like Soma and other gifts, the prayer of the poet is offered to the gods; they enjoy it; they are fortified by it for their heroic deeds; and as man stands in need of the various benefits of the gods, the gods need for their welfare the offerings and especially the prayers of mankind; "prayer is a 'tonic' of the gods"; "Indra for his battles is fortified by prayer" (offered to him); phrases like these occur frequently in the Ṛigveda; thus the idea became more and more prominent that human prayer is a power which surpasses in potency even the might of the gods. In the moments of religious devotion man felt himself raised above his own individuality, felt awakening in himself that metaphysical power on which all worlds with their gods and creatures are dependent. By this curious development (comparable to the history of the Biblical *Λόγος*) Brahman, the old name for prayer, became the most usual name for the creative principle of the world. An old Ṛigvedic question "which was the tree, which was the wood, of which they hewed the earth and heaven"? is repeated in a *Brâhmaṇa* text, and followed by the answer: "The

History of the Brahman

Brahman was the tree, the wood from which they hewed the earth and heaven." Here the term Brahman has become already what it has been through all the following centuries — the most common name for the eternal and changeless principle of the world.

History of the Âtman

9. A better name even than Brahman, and perhaps the best name which philosophy has found in any language to designate the principle of the world, is the word Âtman, which properly is the exact equivalent of the english "Self". Thus Âtman means that which remains if we take away from our person all that is Non-self, foreign, all that comes and passes away; it means "the changeless, inseparable essence of our own Self", and on the other hand the essence of the Self of the whole world. It is not possible, as in the case of Prajâpati and Brahman, to frame a history of the word Âtman. It has no regular development but we see it emerge here and there in proportion as the thinker seeks and finds a more clear-cut expression for the word Brahman to name that being which can never by any means be taken away from us, and therefore forms the only true essence of our nature, our *âtman*, our Self. With this word we have reached the sphere of the Upanishads; we must now say a few words on these most remarkable monuments of ancient Indian literature.

SECOND PERIOD

PHILOSOPHY OF THE UPANISHADS

10. If we compare the Veda and the Bible we may say that the Old Testament is represented in the Veda by all the hymns and *Brâhmaṇa* texts, which serve the purpose of ritual worship. But, as the Old Testament is superseded by the New, so in the Veda all ritual performances with their rewards are declared insufficient and replaced by a higher view of things in those wonderful texts which, forming as a rule the concluding chapters of each Veda, are called Vedânta (end of the Veda) or Upanishads (confidential sitting, secret doctrine). The four Vedas produced different branches or schools, each of which has handed down the common content of the Vedas in a slightly different form. Thus every Vedic school had, besides the Saṃhitâ or collection of verses and formulas, a special Brâhmaṇam as its ritual textbook, and a longer or shorter Upanishad, which forms

The Upanishads of the Veda

its dogmatic text-book. Therefore all the Upanishads treat of the same subject, the doctrine of Brahman or Âtman, and vary only in length and manner of treatment. There are about a dozen Upanishads of the three older Vedas and a great number of later treatises of the same name which are incorporated in the Atharvaveda. Distinguished by its age, length, and intrinsic importance is, before all, the Bṛihadâraṇyaka-Upanishad, and next to it Chândogya-Upanishad. More remarkable for their beauty than for their originality are Kâṭhaka-Upanishad, Muṇḍaka-Upanishad, and others.

Fundamental idea of the Upanishads

11. Two terms, Brahman and Âtman, form almost the only objects of which the Upanishads speak. Very often they are treated as synonyms, but when a difference is noticeable, Brahman is the philosophical principle, as realised in the universe, and *Âtman* the same, as realised in the soul. This presupposed, we might express the fundamental thought of all the Upanishads by the simple equation: —

Brahman = Âtman

that is, Brahman, the power from which all worlds proceed, in which they subsist, and into which they finally return, this eternal, omnipresent, omnipotent power is identical with our âtman, with that in each of us which we must consider as our true Self, the unchangeable essence of our being, our soul. This idea alone secures to the Upanishads an importance reaching far beyond their land and time; for whatever means of unveiling the secrets of Nature a future time may discover, this idea will be true for ever, from this mankind will never depart, — if the mystery of Nature is to be solved, the key of it can be found only there where alone Nature allows us an interior view of the world, that is in ourselves.

Chronology of the Upanishads

12. It can be proved that the Upanishads of the three first Vedas are older generally speaking than the Atharva Upanishads; of the former those in poetic form belong undoubtedly to a later period than those written in the old and simple prose style of the *Brâhmaṇas;* among these again the two oldest are Bṛihadâraṇyaka and Chândogya, which contain the oldest Upanishad texts we possess. There are passages in *Chândogya* which may claim the priority over the parallel texts in *Bṛihadâraṇyaka,* but in most cases it can be clearly proved that passages in *Chândogya* are not only younger than the parallel texts in *Bṛihadâraṇyaka* but even dependent on them; this is evident from the fact that several passages of *Bṛihadâraṇyaka,* recur more or less literally in *Chândogya* but are no longer understood in their original meaning. In this way a careful comparison of the texts leads us to this result that in the whole Upanishad literature there are scarcely any texts older

than those contained in *Bṛih-Up.* 1-4 which are connected with the person of Yâjñavalkya; these either speak of him as is the case in 1, 4 and 2, 4, or reproduce his discourses with adversaries and his friend, the king Janaka, and take up the whole of the third and fourth book. In these passages we have the oldest germ of the doctrine of the Upanishads and consequently of Indian philosophy.

Primitive idealism of the Upanishads

13. In the Yâjñavalkya chapters of Bṛihadâraṇyaka and therefore in the oldest texts of the Upanishads we find as the point of departure of the Upanishad doctrine a very bold idealism comparable to that of Parmenides in Greece, and culminating in the assertion that the *âtman* is the only reality and that nothing exists beyond it. The whole doctrine may be summed up in three statements: —

1. The only reality is the *âtman;*
2. The *âtman* is the subject of knowledge in us;
3. The *âtman* itself is unknowable.

1. All things in heaven and earth, gods, men, and other beings exist only in so far as they form a part of our *âtman;* the *âtman* must be seen, heard, known; he who sees, hears, and knows the *âtman*, knows in it all that exists; as the sounds of a musical instrument cannot be grasped, but he who grasps the instrument, grasps also the sounds, so he who knows the *âtman* knows in it

all that exists; that man is lost and abandoned by gods and men, who believes in the existence of gods and men beyond the *âtman.*

2. This *âtman* is neither more nor less than the seer of seeing, the hearer of hearing, the knower of knowing, in a word the subject of knowledge in us, for this only is our real Self, which can never by any means be taken away from us.

3. The *âtman*, as the subject of knowledge in us, is and remains unknowable in itself. "Thou canst not see the seer of seeing, thou canst not hear the hearer of hearing, thou canst not know the knower of knowing; how could a man know that by which he knows everything, how could he know the knower."

14. The idealism of Yâjñavalkya denies, as we have seen, the existence of the world; but this denial could not be maintained in the long run.

Pantheism

The reality of the world forced itself on the beholder, and the problem was to recognize it without abandoning the truth laid down by the sage Yâjñavalkya. This led to a second stage of development which for want of a better name we may denominate Pantheism. Its chief doctrine is that the world is real, and yet the *âtman* is the only reality, for the world is the *âtman.* This is the most current thesis in the Upanishads and leads to very beautiful conceptions like that in *Chând.* 3, 14: "The *âtman* is my soul in the inner heart, smaller than a barley corn, smaller than a mustard-seed, smaller than a grain of millet; and he again is my soul in the inner heart, larger than the earth, larger than the atmosphere, larger than the heavens and all these worlds."

15. The equation world = âtman, notwithstanding its constant repetition in the Upanishads, is not a transparent one; for the *âtman* is an absolute unity, and the world a plurality. How can they be regarded as identical? This difficulty may have led later on to the attempt to substitute for this incomprehensible identity another relation between *âtman* and world, that of causality. This theory opened the way to a new interpretation of the old myths of creation which consider the principle, Prajâpati or whatever it was, as the cause, and the world as the effect. Accordingly the cosmogonies of the Upanishads teach us that in the beginning the *âtman* alone existed; the *âtman* thought, "I will be manifold, I will send forth worlds", and created all these worlds. Having created them he entered into his creation as the soul, as the Upanishads never fail to emphasize. We have called this standpoint, finding no other name, Cosmogonism; some might propose to call it Theism, but from this it is essentially different. In the theistic view God creates the soul like everything else, but in the case before us the

Cosmogonism

soul is not a creation of the *âtman* but the *âtman* himself, who enters into his creation as the individual soul.

16. The identity of the highest and the individual *âtman*, though perfectly true from the metaphysical standpoint, remains incomprehensible for the empirical view of things; this view distinguishes a plurality of souls different from each other and from the highest *âtman*, the creative power of the universe. This distinction between the highest soul (paramâtman) and the individual souls (jîvâtman) is the characteristic feature of what we may term the theism of certain later Upanishads. It emerges for the first time in *Kâṭhaka* 3, 1, where the two, God and the soul, are contrasted as light and shadow, which intimates that the latter has no reality of its own. But the constantly growing realistic tendencies went on sharpening this contrast, until in the Çvetâçvatara-Up. the highest soul, almighty and all-pervading as it is, is represented as essentially different from the individual soul which, limited and indigent, lives in the heart, smaller than the point of a needle, smaller than the ten-thousandth part of a hair; and this, says the text, "becomes infinity". Even here God, though isolated and severed from the soul, lives together with it in the heart. As two birds living on the same tree, one of which feeds on the fruits of his works, while the other abstains from eating and only looks on;

Theism

thus the individual soul, bewildered by his own impotence and grieving, looks for the help of the highest soul, or rather of his own divine and almighty self.

Atheism

17. Theism distinguishes three entities, a real world, a creative *âtman* and the individual *âtman* dependent on him. This duplication of the *âtman* necessarily had a pernicious influence on one of the two branches, *viz.*, on the highest *âtman*, who in fact had always drawn his vital force from the soul living in us. Separated from this he became altogether superfluous, since the creative powers attributed to him could be transferred without difficulty to the primordial matter. Thus God disappeared and there remained only a primeval creative matter (prakṛiti) and opposed to it a plurality of individual souls (purusha), entangled in it by an inexplicable fate and striving to emancipate themselves from it by means of knowledge. This is exactly the standpoint of the Sâṅkhya system. We see it shoot up more and more exuberantly in the later Upanishads, especially in Maitrâyaṇîya; but its full development is only attained in the post-Vedic period and will be treated later. Before leaving the Veda we have to speak of the moral and eschatological consequences of the Vedic philosophy.

18. In contrast with the Semitic view, the belief in the immortality of the soul has been from the old-

est times a patrimony of the Indo-Germanic race. Even in the oldest hymns of the Ṛigveda the hope is frequently expressed that after death good men will go to the gods to share their happy life. As for the wicked it is their destiny, only darkly hinted at, to fall into a deep abyss and disappear. The first mortal who found the way to the luminous heights of the happy other-world for all the following generations was Yama, who, as king of the blessed dead, sits with them under a leafy tree and passes the time in carousing; the analogous ideas of Jesus when He speaks of sitting at table with Abraham, Isaac, and Jacob in the future state are known to everybody. Different stages of happiness for pious worshippers seem not to have been a part of the oldest creed. In the course of time this was modified and the belief arose that good and evil deeds find their corresponding rewards and punishments in a future life. A very striking passage of a *Brâhmaṇa* says: "Whatever food a man eats in this world, by that food he is eaten in the next world." Among the evils which await the bad man in the world to come we often find mentioned an indefinite fear of dying again and again even in the other world (punarmṛityu). This notion of a repeated death led on to the idea that it must be preceded by a repeated life, and in transferring this repeated

Vedic Eschatology before the Upanishads

living and dying from the world beyond to the earth, the Hindus came finally to that dogma which has been in all subsequent ages more characteristic of India than anything else — the great doctrine of metempsychosis. The first passage where this creed clearly appears is in the *Bṛihadâraṇyaka-Up.*; and it discloses to us also the real motives of the remarkable dogma. Yâjñavalkya, when asked what remains of man after death, takes the interrogator by the hand, leads him from the assembly to a solitary place, and reveals to him there the great secret: "and what they spoke was work, and what they praised was work; verily a man becomes holy by holy works, wicked by wicked works." This passage together with several others proves that the chief motive of the dogma of transmigration was to explain the different destinies of men by the supposition that they are the fruits of merit and demerit in a preceding life.

Development of this Doctrine in the Upanishads

19. A religion, after having come to a better view of things, cannot discard the preceding and less perfect steps of development which have led up to it. Thus the New Testament cannot emancipate itself from the Old Testament and its very different spirit. So too the Upanishads, after having come to the creed of metempsychosis, had to retain at the same time the old Vedic creed

of rewards and punishments in the other world. The two views combined led to a complicated system, which taught a two-fold reward and punishment, the first in the world beyond, the second in a succeeding life on earth. This theory is fully explained in the so-called "doctrine of the Five Fires", an important text found both in *Chând.* 5 and in *Bṛih.* 6. This combined theory of compensation distinguishes three ways after death — (1) the way of the fathers, (2) the way of the gods, and (3) the "third place".

(1) The way of the fathers, destined for the performer of pious works, leads through the smoke of the funeral pyre and a series of "dark" stations to the placid realm of the moon, where the soul in commerce with the gods, enjoys the fruit of its good works, until they are consumed. As soon as the treasure of good works is exhausted, the soul, through the intermediate stations of ether, wind, fog, rain, plant, semen and womb passes to a new human existence, in which once more the good and evil works of the previous life find their reward.

(2) The way of the gods is destined for those who have spent their life in worshipping Brahman. They go through the flame of the funeral pyre and a series of "luminous" stations first to the sun, thence "to the moon, from the moon to the lightning; there is a spirit, he is not like a human being; he leads

them to Brahman. For them there is no return". This passage evidently teaches that by the way of the gods is attained the highest goal, the union with Brahman. The later system, however, teaching that the knower of Brahman stands higher than the worshipper of Brahman, considers this union with Brahman, obtained by worshipping it, only as a step leading to the highest perfection, which the souls united with Brahman obtain only after receiving in it perfect knowledge.

(3) For those who have neither worshipped Brahman nor performed good works the „third place" is destined leading to a new life as lower animals — worms, insects, snakes etc., after a previous punishment in the different hells. This punishment in hell, which is a later addition, is not found in the Upanishads and appears first in the system of the Vedânta.

Liberation by knowledge

20. Transmigration is believed to be just as real as the empirical world. But from a higher point of view empirical reality together with creation and transmigration is only a great illusion; for in truth there is no manifold, no world, but only one being — the Brahman, the âtman. The attainment of this knowledge is the highest aim of man and in its possession consists the final liberation. The knowledge is not the means of liberation, it is liberation itself. He who has attained the conviction "I

am Brahman" has reached with it the knowledge that he in himself is the totality of all that is, and consequently he will not fear anything because there is nothing beyond him; he will not injure anybody, for nobody 'injures himself by himself'. There are, properly speaking, no means of attaining this knowledge; it comes of itself; it is, in the view of the theistic Upanishads, a grace of God. He who has obtained this knowledge continues to live, for he must consume the fruits of his preceding life; but life with its temptations can no longer delude him. By the fire of knowledge his former works are "burnt" and no new works can arise. He knows that his body is not his body, his works are not his works; for he is the totality of the *âtman*, the divine being, and when he dies, "his spirit does not wander any more, for Brahman is he, and into Brahman he is resolved".

"As rivers run and in the deep
Lose name and form and disappear
So goes, from name and form released,
The wise man to the deity."

THIRD PERIOD

POST-VEDIC PHILOSOPHY

General Survey

21. The thoughts of the Upanishads led in the post-Vedic period not only to the two great religions of Buddhism and Jainism but also to a whole series of philosophical systems. Six of these are considered as orthodox, because they are believed to be reconcileable with the Vedic creed, the others are rejected as heretical. The six orthodox systems are: (1) the Sâṅkhyam of Kapila, (2) the Yoga of Patañjali, (3) the Nyâya of Gotama, (4) the Vaiçeshikam of Kaṇâda, (5) the Mîmâṅsâ of Jaimini, (6) the Vedânta of Bâdarâyaṇa. As for the heterodox systems, the most important are Buddhism, Jainism, and the materialistic system of the Cârvâkas; several others are nothing more than the Vedântic views combined with the popular creeds of Vishṇuism or Çivaism. But the six orthodox schools are not philosophical

systems either in the strict sense of the term. The Mîmâṅsâ is only a methodical handbook treating of the various questions arising out of the complicated Vedic ritual. The Yoga is a systematic exposition of the method of attaining union with the *âtman* by means of concentration in oneself. The Nyâya, though it treats incidentally of all kinds of philosophical topics, is properly nothing more than a handbook of logic or better of disputation, furnishing a canon for use in controversies. The Vaiçeshikam, giving a classification of existing things under six categories, is interesting enough, but more from a physical than a philosophical point of view. The only systems of metaphysical importance are the Sâṅkhyam and the Vedânta; but even these are not to be considered as original creations of the philosophical mind, for the common basis of both and with them of Buddhism and Jainism is to be found in the Upanishads; and it is the ideas of the Upanishads which by a kind of degeneration have developed into Buddhism on one side and the Sâṅkhya system on the other. Contrary to both, the later Vedânta of Bâdarâyaṇa and Çaṅkara goes back to the Upanishads and founds on them that great system of the Vedânta which we have to consider as the ripest fruit of Indian wisdom.

22. From the Veda to the later systems leads a philosophical development the history of which, for

want of special documents, must be supplied from the vast bulk of the Mahâbhâratam. Here we find, in the Bhagavadgîtâ (Book vi.), the Sanatsujâtaparvan (Book v. 1565 ff.), the Mokshadharma (Book xii.) and other texts, the materials which, though in an earlier form than that of the *Mahâbhâratam*, have formed the common base of Buddhism and Sâṅkhyam. The philosophical system of the *Mahâbhâratam*, whether we call it epic Sâṅkhyam or realistic *Vedânta*, is the common mother of both. Some scholars maintain that the religion of Buddha is an off-shoot of the Sâṅkhya system, others that Buddhism is anterior to the *Sâṅkhyam*. Both are right. Buddhism certainly precedes what we call now the Sâṅkhya system, but it depends on what is called Sâṅkhyam in the *Mahâbhâratam*. Originally Sâṅkhyam (calculation, reflection) does not mean a certain philosophical system but philosophical enquiry in general; it is the opposite of Yoga, which means the attainment of the *âtman* by means of concentration in oneself. The words are thus used where they occur for the first time (*Çvet.* 6, 13), and it is an open question, demanding further research, whether not only in the *Bhagavadgîtâ* but also throughout the *Mahâbhâratam* the words *Sâṅkhyam* and *Yoga* are not so much names of philosophical systems as general terms for the two methods of reflection and concentration. Without entering into details we may

The Philosophy of the Epic Period

say that even in the *Mahâbhâratam* the primordial matter (*prakṛiti*) is opposed to a plurality of souls *(purusha)*; but both are more or less slightly dependent on Brahman as on the highest principle. This is the starting point both of the later Sâṅkhyam which rejects Brahman as the connecting link, and of Buddhism which denies not only God but also the soul.

23. The success of Buddhism in India was due in part to the overwhelming personality of its founder, in part to the breaking down of caste prejudices by which he opened the road to salvation to the great masses of the population. Only in small measure did the Buddhism owe this success to the originality of its ideas, for almost all its essential theories had their predecessors in the Vedic and epic periods. The fundamental idea of Buddhism, laid down in the four holy truths, is this — that we can extinguish the pains of existence only by extinguishing our thirst for existence. The same idea is put forth in the 12 Nidânas, which by a series of steps go back from the pains of life to the thirst for life and from this to ignorance as the ultimate cause of thirst and pain altogether. We see in these and many other Buddhistic ideas only a new form of what Yâjñavalkya teaches in the *Bṛih.-Up.* and if Buddhism in its opposition to the Brahmanical creed goes so far as to deny soul, this denial is only apparent, since Buddhism maintains

Buddhism

the theory of transmigration effected by karman, the work of the preceding existence. This *karman* must have in every case an individual bearer and that is what the Upanishads call the *âtman* and what the Buddhists inconsistently deny. A common feature of Buddhism and Sâṅkhyam is that they both regard pain as the starting point of philosophical enquiry, thus clearly showing the secondary character of both. For philosophy has its root in the thirst for knowledge and it is a symptom of decadence in India as in Greece when it begins to be considered as a remedy for the pains of life.

The Later Sâñkhya System

24. There are many other features in the Sâñkhya system which show clearly that it is not, as has been generally held up to the present, the original creation of an individual philosophical genius, but only the final result of a long process of degeneration, as has already been shown. The theism of the Upanishads had separated the highest soul from the individual soul, opposing to them a primordial matter. After the elimination of the highest soul there remained two principles —(1) prakṛiti, primeval matter, and (2) a plurality of purushas or subjects of knowledge. This dualism, as the starting-point of the Sâṅkhya system, is in itself quite incomprehensible; it becomes intelligible only by its development as shown before. The aim of man is the emancipation of the *purusha* from the *prakṛiti;* and this is attained by the knowledge

that *purusha* and *prakṛiti* are totally different, and that all the pains of life, being only modifications of *prakṛiti*, do not affect the *purusha* in the least. To awaken this consciousness in the purusha, prakṛiti unfolds its essence to it anew in every life, producing by gradual evolution the cosmic intellect (Mahân or Buddhi), from this the principle of individuation (Ahaṅkâra), from this mind, organs of sense, and the rudiments, and from the latter material objects. The *purusha* beholds this evolution of *prakṛiti*; if he understands that *prakṛiti* is different from himself he is emancipated, if not he remains in the circle of transmigration and suffering. The whole system seems to be based on an original assumption that there is only one *purusha* and one *prakṛiti* by the separation of which the final aim is attained for both. The pretended plurality of *purushas* looks like a later addition; and we do not understand how the one and indivisible *prakṛiti* develops its being before every single *purusha* again and again to help him in his emancipation, if there always remains an innumerable quantity of unemancipated *purushas*. If we add to this the fact that all the other elements of the system including the three guṇas can be derived from the Upanishad doctrine, we can no longer hesitate to admit that the whole Sâṅkhya system is nothing but a result of the degeneration of the Vedânta by means of the growth of realistic tendencies. There seems to have been a time when Vedântic thought lived only in this realistic form of the Sâṅkhya; for when the Yoga took the form of a philosophical system it was built up on the very inconvenient base of the Sâṅkhya system, probably because at that time no other base was available.

The System of the Vedânta

25. The genesis of the Vedânta-system, represented by Bâdarâyaṇa and Çaṅkara, has many analogies with the Reformation in the Christian Church. In the same way as Luther and others rejected the various traditions of the medieval Church and based the Protestant creed on the pure word of the Bible, so Çaṅkara (born 788 A. D.) rejected the changes in Vedic doctrine brought about by Buddhism and Sâṅkhya and founded the great system that bears his name on the holy word of the Upanishads alone; but in doing this a great difficulty arose; for the Upanishads, the words of which are in the view of Çaṅkara a divine revelation, contain not only the pure idealism of Yâjñavalkya but also its later modifications such as pantheism, cosmogonism and theism. In meeting this difficulty Çaṅkara exhibits great philosophical astuteness, which may serve as a model for Christian theology in future times; he distinguishes throughout an esoteric system (paravidyâ) containing a sublime philosophy, and an exoteric system (aparavidyâ) embracing under the wide mantle of a theological creed all the fanciful imaginings which spring in course of time from the original idealism. The exo-

teric system gives a description of the Brahman in the richest colours, treating it in part as the pantheistic soul of the world, and in part as a personal god; it gives a full account of the periodical creation and reabsorption of the world and of the never-ending circle of transmigration, etc. The esoteric system on the contrary maintains with Yâjñavalkya that Brahman, or the *âtman* is absolutely unknowable and attainable only by the concentration of *yoga*, that there is from the highest standpoint neither creation nor world, neither transmigration nor plurality of souls, and that complete liberation is reached by him and by him alone who has awakened to the beatific consciousness, expressed in the words of the Upanishads: "Aham Brahma asmi" (I am Brahman).

Thus the Indians in their Vedânta possess a theological and philosophical system satisfying not only the wants of the people, but also the demands of a mind accessible to true knowledge only in its purest form.

ON THE
PHILOSOPHY OF THE VEDÂNTA
IN ITS
RELATIONS TO OCCIDENTAL METAPHYSICS

AN ADDRESS DELIVERED BEFORE THE BOMBAY
BRANCH OF THE ROYAL ASIATIC SOCIETY
25. FEBRUARY 1893.

INTRODUCTION

ON my journey through India I have noticed with satisfaction, that in philosophy till now our brothers in the East have maintained a very good tradition, better perhaps, than the more active but less contemplative branches of the great Indo-Aryan family in Europe, where Empirism, Realism and their natural consequence, Materialism, grow from day to day more exuberantly, whilst metaphysics, the very centre and heart of serious philosophy, are supported only by the few who have learned to brave the spirit of the age.

In India the influence of this perverted and perversive spirit of our age has not yet overthrown in religion and philosophy the good traditions of the great ancient time. It is true, that most of the ancient *darçana*'s even in India find only an historical interest; followers of the Sâṅkhya-System occur rarely; Nyâya is cultivated mostly as an intellectual sport and exercise, like grammar or mathematics, — but the Vedânta is, now as in the ancient time, living in the mind and heart of every thoughtful Hindoo. It is true, that even here in the sanctuary of Vedântic metaphysics, the realistic tendencies, natural to man, have penetrated, producing the misinterpreting variations of Çaṅkara's Advaita, known under the names Viçishṭâdvaita, Dvaita, Çuddhâdvaita of Râmânuja, Mâdhva, Vallabha, — but India till now has not yet been seduced by their voices, and of hundred Vedântins (I have it from a well informed man, who is himself a zealous adversary of Çaṅkara and follower of Râmânuja) fifteen perhaps adhere to Râmânuja, five to Mâdhva, five to Vallabha, and seventy-five to Çaṅkarâchârya. „

This fact may be for poor India in so many misfortunes a great consolation; for the eternal interests are higher than the temporary ones; and the System of the Vedânta, as founded on the Upanishads and Vedânta Sûtras and accomplished by Çaṅkara's commentaries on them, — equal in rank to Plato and Kant — is one of the most valuable products of the genius of mankind in his researches of the eternal truth, — as I propose to show now by a short sketch of Çaṅkara's Advaita and by comparing its principal doctrines with the best that occidental philosophy has produced till now.

Taking the Upanishads, as Çaṅkara does, for revealed truth with absolute authority, it was not an easy task to build out of their materials a consistent philosophical system, for the Upanishads are in Theology, Kosmology and Psychology full of the hardest contradictions. So in many passages the nature of Brahman is painted in various and luxuriant colours, and again we read, that the nature of Brahman is quite unattainable to human words, to human understanding; — so wc meet sometimes long reports explaining how the world has been created by Brahman, and again we are told, that there is no world besides Brahman, and all variety of things is mere error and illusion; — so we have fanciful descriptions of the Saṃsâra, the way of the wandering soul up to the heaven and back to the earth, and again we read, that there is no Saṃsâra, no variety of souls at all, but only one Âtman, who is fully and totally residing in every being.

Çaṅkara in these difficulties created by the nature of his materials, in face of so many contradictory doctrines, which he was not allowed to decline and yet could not admit altogether, — has found a wonderful device, which deserves the attention, perhaps the imitation of the Christian dogmatists in their embarassments. He constructs out of the materials of the Upanishads two systems, one esoteric, philosophical (called by him *nirguṇâ vidyâ*, sometimes *pâramârthikâ avasthâ*) containing the metaphysical truth for the few ones, rare in all times and countries, who are able to understand it; and another exoteric, theological (*saguṇâ vidyâ, vyâvahârikî avasthâ*) for the general public, who want images, not abstract truth, worship, not meditation.

I shall now point out briefly the two systems, esoteric and exoteric, in pursuing and confronting them through the four chief parts, which Çaṅkara's system contains, and every complete philosophical system must contain:—

I. Theology, the doctrine of God or of the philosophical principle.

II. Cosmology, the doctrine of the world.

III. Psychology, the doctrine of the soul.

IV. Eschatology, the doctrine of the last things, the things after death.

CHAPTER I
THEOLOGY

The Upanishads swarm with fanciful and contradictory descriptions of the nature of Brahman. He is the all-pervading âkâça, is the purusha in the sun, the purusha in the eye; his head is the heaven, his eyes are sun and moon, his breath is the wind, his footstool the earth; he is infinitely great as soul of the universe and infinitely small as the soul in us; he is in particular the *içvara*, the personal God, distributing justly reward and punishment according to the deeds of man. All these numerous descriptions are collected by Çaṅkara under the wide mantle of the exoteric theology, the *saguṇâ vidyâ* of Brahman, consisting of numerous "vidyâs" adapted for approaching the eternal being not by the way of knowledge but by the way of worshipping, and having each its particular fruits. Mark, that also the conception of God as a personal being, an *icvara*, is merely exoteric and does not give us an adequate knowledge of the Âtman; — and indeed, when we consider what is personality, how narrow in its limitations, how closely connected which egotism, the counter part of godly essence, who might think so low of God, to impute him personality?

In the sharpest contrast to these exoteric vidyâs stands the esoteric *nirguṇâ vidyâ* of the Âtman; and its fundamental tenet is the absolute inaccessibility of God to human thoughts and words;

अविज्ञातं विजानतां
विज्ञातमविजानताम्.

and again:

यतो वाचो निवर्त्तन्ते
अप्राप्य मनसा सह.

and the celebrated formula occurring so often in Bṛihadâraṇyaka-Upanishad: *neti! neti!* viz., whatever attempt you make to know the Âtman, whatever description you give of him, I always say: *na iti, na iti,* it is not so, it is not so! Therefore the wise Bâhva, when asked by the king Vâshkalin, to explain the Brahman, kept silence. And when the king repeated his request again and again, the ṛishi broke out into the answer: "I tell it you, but you don't understand it; *çânto 'yam âtmâ,* this Âtmâ is silence!" We know it now by the Kantian philosophy, that the answer of Bâhva was correct, we know it, that the very organisation of our intellect (which is bound once for ever to its innate forms of perception, space, time, and causality) excludes us from a knowledge of the spaceless, timeless, godly reality for ever and ever. And yet the Âtman, the only godly being is not unattainable to us, is even not far from us, for we have it fully and totally in ourselves as our own metaphysical entity; and here, when returning from the outside and apparent world to the deepest secrets of our own nature, we may come to God, not by knowledge, but by *anubhava*, by absorption into our own self. There is a great difference between knowledge, in which subject and object are distinct from each other, and anubhava, where subject and object coincide in the same. He who by anubhava comes to the great intelligence, "*aham brahma asmi*", obtains a state called by Çaṅkara *Saṃrâdhanam*, accomplished satisfaction; and indeed, what might he desire, who feels and knows himself as the sum and totality of all existence!

CHAPTER II

COSMOLOGY

Here again we meet the distinction of exoteric and esoteric doctrine, though not so clearly severed by Çaṅkara as in other parts of his system.

The exoteric Cosmology according to the natural but erroneous realism *(avidyâ)* in which we are born, considers this world as the reality, and can express its entire dependency on Brahman only by the mythical way of a creation of the world by Brahman. So a temporal creation of the world, even as in the Christian documents, is also taught in various and well-known passages of the Upanishads. But such a creation of the material world by an immaterial cause, performed in a certain point of time after an eternity elapsed uselessly, is not only against the demands of human reason and natural science, but also against another important doctrine of the Vedânta, which teaches and must teach (as we shall see hereafter) the "beginninglessness of the migration of souls", *saṃsârasya anâditvam.* Here the expedient of Çaṅkara is very clever and worthy of imitation. Instead of the temporary creation once for ever of the Upanishads, he teaches that the world in great periods is created and reabsorbed by Brahman (referring to the misunderstood verse of the Ṛigveda: सूर्याचन्द्रमसौ धाता यथापूर्वमकल्पयत्); this mutual creation and reabsorption lasts from eternity, and no creation can be allowed by our system to be the first and that for good reasons, as we shall see just now.—If we ask: *Why* has God created the world? the answers to this question are generally very unsatisfactory. For his own glorification? How may we attribute to him so much vanity!—For his particular amusement? But he was an eternity without this plaything!—For love of mankind? How may he love a thing before it exists, and how may it be called love, to create millions for misery and eternal pain!—The Vedânta has a better answer. The never ceasing new-creation of the world is a moral necessity connected with the central and most valuable doctrine of the exoteric Vedânta, the doctrine of Saṃsâra.

Man, says Çaṅkara, is like a plant. He grows, flourishes and at the end he dies; but not totally. For as the plant, when dying, leaves behind it the seed, from which, according to its quality, a new plant grows, — so man, when dying, leaves his *karma*, the good and bad works of his life, which must be rewarded and punished in another life after this. No life can be the first, for it is the fruit of previous actions, nor the last, for its actions must be expiated in a next following life. So the Saṃsâra is without beginning and without end, and the new creation of the world after every absorption into Brahman is a moral necessity. I need not point out, in India less than anywhere, the high value of this doctrine of Saṃsâra as a consolation in the afflictions as a moral agent in the temptations of life, — I have to say here only, that the Saṃsâra, though not the absolute truth, is a mythical representative of a truth which in itself is unattainable to our intellect; mythical is this theory of metempsychosis only in so far as it invests in the forms of space and time what really is spaceless and timeless, and therefore beyond the reach of our understanding. So the Saṃsâra is just so far from the truth, as the *saguṇâ vidyâ* is from the *nirguṇâ vidyâ*; it is the eternal truth itself, but (since we cannot conceive it otherwise) the truth in an allegorical form, adapted to our human understanding. And this is the character of the whole exoteric Vedânta, whilst the esoteric doctrine tries to find out the philosophical, the absolute truth.

And so we come to the esoteric Cosmology, whose simple doctrinc is this, that in reality there is no manifold world, but only Brahman, and that what we consider as the world, is a mere illusion (*mâyâ)* similar to a *mṛigatṛishṇikâ*, which disappears when we approach it, and not more to be feared than the rope, which we took in the darkness for a serpent. There are, as you see, many similes in the Vedânta, to illustrate the illusive character of this world, but the best of them is perhaps, when Çaṅkara compares our life with a long dream; — a man whilst dreaming does not doubt oft the reality of the dream, but this reality disappears in the moment of awakening, to give place to a truer reality, which we were not aware of whilst dreaming. The life a dream! this has been the thought of many wise men from Pindar and Sophocles to Shakspere and Calderon de la Barca, but nobody has better explained this idea, than Çaṅkara. And indeed, the moment when we die may be to nothing so similar as to the awakening from a long and heavy dream; it may be, that then heaven and earth are blown away like the nightly phantoms of the dream, and what then may stand before us? or rather in us? Brahman, the eternal reality, which was hidden to us till then by this dream of life! — This world is mâyâ, is illusion; is not the very reality, that is the deepest thought of the esoteric Vedânta, attained not by calculating *tarka* but by *anubhava,* by returning from this variegated world to the deep recess of our own self *(Âtman)*.

Do so, if you can, and you will get aware of a reality very different from empirical reality, a timeless, spaceless, changeless reality, and you will feel and experience that whatever is outside of this only true reality, is mere appearance, is mâyâ, is a dream! — This was the way the Indian thinkers went, and by a similar way, shown by Parmenides, Plato came to the same truth, when knowing and teaching that this world is a world of shadows, and that the reality is not in these shadows, but behind them. The accord here of Platonism and Vedantism is wonderful, but both have grasped this great metaphysical truth by intuition; their tenet is true, but they are not able to prove it, and in so far they are defective. And here a great light and assistance to the Indian and the Greek thinker comes from the philosophy of Kant, who went quite another way, not the Vedantic and Platonic way of intuition, but the way of abstract reasoning and scientific proof. The great work of Kant is an analysis of human mind, not in the superficial way of Locke, but going to the very bottom of it. And in doing so, Kant found, to the surprise of the world and of himself, that three essential elements of this outside world, *viz.*, space, time, and causality, are not, as we naturally believe, eternal fundamentals of an objective reality, but merely subjective innate perceptual forms of our own intellect.

This has been proved by Kant and by his great disciple Schopenhauer with mathematical evidence, and I have given these proofs (the base of all scientific metaphysics) in the shortest and clearest form in my "Elemente der Metaphysik" — a book which I am resolved now to get translated into English*, for the benefit not of the Europeans (who may learn German) but of my brothers in India, who will be greatly astonished to find in Germany the scientific substruction of their own philosophy, of the Advaita Vedânta! For Kant has demonstrated, that space, time and causality are not objective realities, but only subjective forms of our intellect, and the unavoidable conclusion is this, that the world, as far as it is extended in space, running on in time, ruled throughout by causality, in so far is merely a representation of my mind and nothing beyond it. You see the concordance of Indian, Greek and German metaphysics; the world is mâyâ, is illusion, says *Çaṅkara;* — it is a world of shadows, not of realities, says *Plato*; — it is "appearance only, not the thing in itself", says *Kant.* Here we have the same doctrine in three different parts of the world, but the scientific proofs of it are not in Çaṅkara, not in Plato, but only in Kant.

---

* The Elements of Metaphysics, translated into English by C. M. Duff. London 1894.

CHAPTER III
PSYCHOLOGY

Here we convert the order and begin with the esoteric Psychology, because it is closely connected with the esoteric Cosmology and its fundamental doctrine: the world is *mâyâ.* All is illusive, with one exception, with the exception of my own Self, of my Âtman. My Âtman cannot be illusive, as Çaṅkara shows, anticipating the "*cogito, ergo sum*" of Descartes, — for he who would deny it, even in denying it, witnesses its reality. But what is the relation between my individual soul, the Jîva-Âtman, and the highest soul, the Parama-Âtman or Brahman? Here Çaṅkara, like a prophet, foresees the deviations of Râmânuja, Mâdhva and Vallabha and refutes them in showing, that the Jîva cannot be a part of Brahman (Râmânuja), because Brahman is without parts (for it is timeless and spaceless, and all parts are either successions in time or co-ordinations in space, — as we may add), — neither a different thing from Brahman (Mâdhva), for Brahman is *ekam eva advitîyam*, as we may experience by *anubhava*, — nor a metamorphose of Brahman (Vallabha), for Brahman is unchangeable (for, as we know now by Kant, it is out of causality). The conclusion is, that the Jîva being neither a part nor a different thing, nor a variation of Brahman, must be the Paramâtman fully and totally himself, a conclusion made equally by the Vedântin Çaṅkara, by the Platonic Plotinos, and by the Kantian Schopenhauer. But Çaṅkara in his conclusions goes perhaps further than any of them. If really our soul, says he, is not a part of Brahman but Brahman himself, then all the attributes of Brahman, all-pervadingness, eternity, all-migthiness (scientifically spoken: exemption of space, time, causality) are ours; *aham brahma asmi*, I am Brahman, and consequently I am all-pervading (spaceless), eternal (timeless), almigthy (not limited in my doing by causality). But these godly qualities are hidden in me, says Çaṅkara, as the fire is hidden in the wood, and will appear only after the final deliverance.

What is the cause of this concealment of my godly nature? The Upâdhi's, answers Çaṅkara, and with this answer we pass from the esoteric to the exoteric psychology. The Upâdhi's are manas and indriya's, prâṇa with its five branches, sûkshmam çarîram, — in short, the whole psychological apparatus, which together with a factor changeable from birth to birth, with my karman, accompanies my Âtman in all his ways of migration, without infecting his godly nature, as the crystal is not infected by the colour painted over it. But wherefrom originate these Upâdhi's? They form of course part of the *mâyâ*, the great world-illusion, and like *mâyâ* they are based on our innate *avidyâ* or ignorance, a merely negative power and yet strong enough to keep us from our godly existence. But now, from where comes this *avidyâ*, this primeval cause of ignorance, sin, and misery? Here all philosophers in India and Greece and everywhere have been defective, until Kant came to show us that the whole question is inadmissible. You ask for the cause of *avidyâ*, but it has no cause; for causality goes only so far as this world of the Saṃsâra goes, connecting each link of it with another, but never beyond Saṃsâra and its fundamental characteristic, the *avidyâ*. In enquiring after a cause of *avidyâ* with *mâyâ*, Saṃsâra and Upâdhi's, you abuse, as Kant may teach us, your innate mental organ of causality to penetrate into a region for which it is not made, and where it is no more available. The fact is, that we are here in ignorance, sin and misery, and that we know the way out of them, but the question of a cause for them is senseless.

CHAPTER IV

ESCHATOLOGY

And now a few words about this way out of the Saṃsâra, and first about the exoteric theory of it. In the ancient time of the hymns there was no idea of Saṃsâra but only rewards in heaven and (somewhat later) punishments in a dark region *(padam gabhîram)*, the precursor of the later hells. Then the deep theory of Saṃsâra came up, teaching rewards and punishment in the form of a new birth on earth. The Vedânta combines both theories, and so it has a double expiation, first in heaven and hell, and then again in a new existence on the earth. This double expiation is different (1) for performers of good works, going the *pitṛiyâna*, (2) for worshippers of the saguṇam brahma, going the *devayâna*, (3) for wicked deeds, leading to what is obscurely hinted at in the Upanishads as the *tṛitîyaṃ sthânam*, the third place. (1) The *pitṛiyâna* leads through a succession of dark spheres to the moon, there to enjoy the fruit of the good works and, after their consumption, back to an earthly existencc. (2) The *devayâna* leads through a set of brighter spheres to Brahman, without returning to the earth (तेषां न पुनरावृत्तिः). But this Brahman is only saguṇam brahma, the object of worshipping, and its true worshippers, though entering into this saguṇam brahma without returning, have to wait in it until they get *moksha* by obtaining *samyagdarçanam*, the full knowledge of the nirguṇam brahma. (3) The *tṛitîyaṃ sthânam*, including the later theories of hells, teaches punishment in them, and again punishment by returning to earth in the form of lower castes, animals, and plants. All these various and fantastical ways of Saṃsâra are considered as true, quite as true as this world is, but not more. For the whole world and the whole way of Saṃsâra is valid and true for those only who are in the *avidyâ*, not for those who havc overcome it, as we have to show now.

The esoteric Vedânta does not admit the reality of the world nor of the Saṃsâra, for the only reality is Brahman, seized in ourselves as our own Âtman. The knowledge of this Âtman, the great intelligence: "*aham brahma asmi*", does not produce *moksha* (deliverance), but is *moksha* itself. Then we obtain what the Upanishad say:

भिद्यते हृदयग्रन्थिः
छिद्यन्ते सर्वसंशयाः।
क्षीयन्ते चास्य कर्माणि
तस्मिन्दृष्टे परावरे ॥

When seeing Brahma as the highest and the lowest everywhere, all knots of our heart, all sorrows are split, all doubts vanish, and our works become nothing. Certainly no man can live without doing work, and so also the *Jîvanmukta;* but he knows, that all these works are illusive, as this whole world is, and therefore they do not adhere to him nor produce for him a new life after death. — And what kind of work may such a man do? — People have often reproached the Vedânta with being defective in morals, and indeed, the Indian genius is too contemplative to speak much of deeds; but the fact is nevertheless, that the highest and purest morality is the immediate consequence of the Vedânta. The Gospels fix quite correctly as the highest law of morality: "love your neighbour as yourselves." But why should I do so, since by the order of nature I feel pain and pleasure only in myself, not in my neighbour? The answer is not in the Bible (this venerable book being not yet quite free of Semitic realism), but it is in the Veda, is in the great formula "*tat tvam asi*", which gives in three words metaphysics and morals altogether. You shall love your neighbour as yourselves, — because y o u a r e your neighbour, and mere illusion makes you believe, that your neighbour is something different from yourselves. Or in the words of the Bhagavadgîtâḥ: he, who knows himself in everything and everything in himself, will not injure himself by himself, *na hinasti âtmanâ âtmânam*. This is the sum and tenor of all morality, and this is the standpoint of a man knowing himself as Brahman. He feels himself everything, — so he will not desire anything, for he has whatever can be had; — he feels himself everything, — so he will not injure anything, for nobody injures himself. He lives in the world, is surrounded by its illusions but not deceived by them: like the man suffering from *timira*, who sees two moons but knows that there is one only, so the Jîvanmukta sees the manifold world and cannot get rid of seeing it, but he knows, that there is only one being, Brahman, the Âtman, his own Self, and he verifies it by his deeds of pure disinterested morality. And so he expects his end, as the potter expects the end of the twirling of his wheel, after the vessel is ready. And then, for him, when death comes, no more Saṃsâra: न तस्य प्राणा उत्क्रामन्ति । ब्रह्म एव सन् ब्रह्म अप्येति! He enters into brahman, like the streams into the ocean:

यथा नद्यः स्यन्दमानाः समुद्रे
अस्तं गच्छन्ति नामरूपे विहाय ।
तथा विद्वान् नामरूपाद्विमुक्तः
परात्परं पुरुषमुपैति दिव्यम् ॥

he leaves behind him *nâma* and *rûpam*, he leaves behind him *individuality*, but he does not leave behind him his *Âtman*, his Self. It is not the falling of the drop into the infinite ocean, it is the whole ocean, becoming free from the fetters of ice, returning from its frozen state to that what it is really and has never ceased to be, to its own all-pervading, eternal, all-mighty nature.

And so the Vedânta, in its pure and unfalsified form, ist he strongest support of pure morality, is the greatest consolation in the sufferings of life and death,—Indians, keep to it!—

INDEX
OF NAMES AND SUBJECTS.